Creative Writing & Content Marketing

Interesting Articles That Sell

Contents

Introduction

If you run your own website, write your own blog, or simply have goods to sell, then you will be consistently on the hunt for more Internet traffic, which means looking for fresh *'**Interesting Content**'* for your business.

If you run your own Internet business then you will agree that traffic is the hardest aspect to marketing your goods, it is the lifeblood of any Internet business.

Without the ability to attract a large volume of traffic and regardless of how good your product or services are...**no one will ever be any the wiser to their existence**.

And it's a sad fact that year-upon-year, millions of website owners and Internet businesses never experience any real significant amounts of traffic, finding themselves out of business.

However, there is a range of opportunity's at your disposal, which can help you increase your website, or blogs... traffic.

Internet businesses have known for years that one of the best ways to create traffic is to write great content... but not just any content, it has to be 'SPECIALLY WRITTEN CONTENT'!

It must be engaging, interesting, and informative, because the Internet is awash with millions of articles expressing tons of tips, facts, including help.

You are able to excess uncountable services, books and products... if your content doesn't meet your readers expectations, ***it won't get read***.

Unfortunately, not all the methods available to you are equal and the trick is to know, which ones to use and, which ones to leave well alone.

For example, there was a time when writing **'Content'**, then submitting it to article directories, would flood your website with hordes of visitors to buy your goods... people just loved to read content about almost anything you can think of.

Content feed upon the insatiable appetite people had for information; people are desperate for tips, advice, and help on almost any subject you can think of.

And they would pay a handsome price too.

Writing content and then distributing it around the Internet was without doubt one of the best, free, and easiest ways to increase your Internet traffic... and Google loved them too.

You may have read that writing content will no longer work, and unfortunately, it's true to an extent. Like all good things that appear on the Internet, people end-up abusing the system and losing it.

Google's destroyed most article directories, because people where producing content, spinning the content into thousands of copies that said the same thing.

You couldn't even read some of the content, but still it was submitting all over the Internet...they were full of scummy back links too.

But don't think that writing content will lessen your impact, because in reality, the rewards can be very considerable.

You need to ask yourself a very simple question... *"If Internet Webmasters are still using these techniques to promote their businesses, then why shouldn't I"*?

Well Webmasters still use articles to market their websites and programs to great effect, even today?

You should keep submitting your articles to article directors to a minimum, because it may harm your Website rankings...

Google doesn't like article directories and will mark down your site in their Google Serps.

And don't think you can hide from Google.

They read every word you submit on the Internet, every piece of content, eBooks, emails, landing pages, opt-in pages, news releases, blogs, and Website pages.

If you can name it Google will have read and noted it.

That's what Google does; it's built an empire around information supplied by websites, blogs, and articles. Writers, they do all the hard work.

It's their experiences, misfortunes, loves, business ideas, regrets, newsletters, and 'How' to books, Google supplies you when you search the Internet.

Whatever you do, don't ever be tempted to open a Gmail or Google+ account, because Google will use your personal information to its own advantage and not yours.

'Why' Should You Bother to Write Content

The idea behind writing content is to introduce new, unique, and helpful information to your customers, in the hope they will visit your Website, blog, or promotion... encouraging SEO, traffic, comments, shares, subscribers, and buyers.

In order to write content, which you can distribute around the Internet will involve the use of *'Social Media'* websites.

'Social Media' Websites are portals that have the ability to host a large collection of text and/or content, which invites the general public to access and read your message.

To make it easier to find your content in their websites, many 'Social Media' sites place your content into a category, popular categories include: how to, health, cars, travel, keep fit, weight loss, businesses, Internet, computers, software, travel, and so on.

Where to Submit Your Content

Social media Websites include:

http://twitter.com   https://www.pinterest.com
https://www.google.co.uk   https://www.youtube.com

https://uk.linkedin.com   https://www.facebook.com
http://instagram.com

Other places are **'Blogger'** communities. They are a great place where you can connect with other individuals who are enthusiastically writing about, or looking for information on your niche or topic.

Blogger communities include:

http://triberr.com   http://www.socialbuzzclub.com
http://bizbloggingbuzz.com   http://myblogguest.com
http://viralcontentbuzz.com

Also Bookmark Websites: Top of my list is:

http://digg.com   http://reddit.com
http://www.stumbleupon.com   http://www.scoop.it
https://delicious.com   https://onlywire.com
http://www.socialmarker.com
http://socialadr.com

Just remember the more content you distribute throughout the Internet the more traffic you get back to your Website = more *'Profit'*... but it MUST be 'Unique'!

There are 100's of other sites you could submit your content to, simply do searches on Google for more listings.

Just be careful to read the small print, and take a look at their terms of condition.

Not only are there a ton of places to submit your content to, but there are many forms your content can be delivered in.

For example, not only do you have your standard text for the Social and Book Marketing Websites, books, magazines, how-to reports, journals, manuals, reviews, news papers, press releases, but there are also PDF, kindle, and videos to name a few.

As you can see writing content is part of any and ALL businesses, but the time has now come to devote more time to **'How'** you write your content instead of **'What'** you write.

The media world is changing and you need to embrace this new shifting transformation before it's too late.

Internet Content Gives You a Very Special Advantage Over Other Forms of Writing

The real advantage to writing content for the Internet is your ability to place links into your story, these links will point back to wherever you want your customers to go.

It could be your website, blog, landing page, sales page, opt-in page, affiliate promotion, other content, even an acquaintances website or blog, anyway you want your reader to go.

This ability to place a link anywhere within your article is known as a 'back link', more on this subject later.

But don't go mad and saturate your content with loads of back links, because Google will disregard them... place about three links in total.

Becoming a Successful Writer

If you want to be anywhere close to becoming a successful Website or Blog writer, then your content must be interesting, engaging, and above all... Helpful!

They must be the type of content that your readers just can't put down until they finish.

Most writers tend to write in a more traditional, and boring fashion; content that their readers probably never bother to read right through to the end.

If you don't want this to happen to you then your first instinct should be to... *'Analyse the way in, which you write'.*

I don't know about you, but I like to enjoy what I read… even if it's technical stuff.

This is **'why'** it is extremely important you learn to write captivating content.

If you are looking to become successful at writing content, then it's essential to keep both eyes on the ball.

Never lose sight of the fact that the subject of your content **isn't** as important as the way that your content is written, having said that, it does come in a close second.

And this is **'Why'** you should always write content that interest you <u>first</u>, because if you're not interested in the subject matter then it's almost impossible to write exciting content.

Of course it's very important that they cover subjects that will draw in readers, and readers from all walks of life.

'How' to Increase Interest And Traffic to Your Content - Brainstorming

As mentioned earlier, you should always write about subjects that you find interesting first.

Having passion in your subject will make it a lot easier to write more livelier, exciting, and colourful content.

But it's also absolutely imperative that you bear in mind that many of your readers will not have the same interests as you do.

So when writing your content, make sure not to forget to put your reader's interests above your own, this should always be your top priority.

This is such an important aspect of writing excellent content. It's fine if what you have written lights up your night sky, but this is not the reason for writing your article.

Therefore, I urge you to broaden your horizons by writing about topics that are outside of your comfort zone.

For example, why not consider writing articles that cover some hot 'Topic', but also encompasses your subject.

To begin with, you may find this process a bit daunting, but there are a number of different approaches you can take to lessen this affect, brainstorming, for example.

Brainstorming

Let's take a look at brainstorming and what it involves.

I personally use brainstorming to help me build and develop my article ideas.

It's one of the most essential skills you simply must learn to develop, and to your highest level.

So how do I use brainstorming to develop my ideas I hear you asking?

Brainstorming helps me to create, develop, and then build solutions to a given problem.

Unfortunately, the term brainstorming builds a misleading picture of using your brain to conjure up unknown ideas.

Although it's true, you need to use your brain to an

extent, we also need the use of tools to achieve an effective solution to make this whole process worthwhile.

One of your best, free, and accessible tools is the Internet... no surprise there!

As a matter of fact, when writing articles you are unfamiliar with, you will come to realize that the Internet is in fact your best source of information.

In order to attract the maximum number of readers to your content, your articles should focus on subjects that are best described as hot 'Topics'.

A hot 'topic' could be considered to be some recent 'news report', or a highly debated subject, a popular product/service, or gossip regarding a well-liked celebrity.

Of course, which hot topic you decide to write about is yours to make, however, it's useful to know that many Internet surfers do enjoy reading articles that focus on hot products and services... sometimes referred to as... *'Product reviews'*!

Should you decide that you would like to write product reviews then you may want to examine popular shopping websites to gain information, images, and even videos of the products you would like to review?

Two of the most popular websites to visit will include 'http://ebay.com and http/:www.amazon.com. I love these websites, because they very often list fashion -

able **'Big ticket'** items right on their home pages.

These big ticket items are the ones that are the most searched for items, or top purchased items on their website.

Writing a focused product review on such high ticket products will help to bring in maximum profits to your business.

Remember, these are items that are in high demand and will bring targeted readers **'who'** really want to read your content, increasing your traffic and above all, your profits.

This explains exactly what brainstorming is all about. It's all about finding those hot stories, articles, products, etc; your readers are actively seeking and want to read.

Thoroughly research, examine, and know your subject, then create an outline for yourself, which can be continuously updated or developed.

Don't rush this process, it's too important to get wrong.

Remember, whatever you finally end up with will remain on the Internet for many years to come and you want your content to be as powerful in the future, as it is today.

If you can afford to purchase the product or service you are interested in promoting then why not purchase the product and tested it out for yourself.

Some of the most successful product reviews are

written by people who actually purchased and used the product... an idea you may want to keep in mind.

It's not hard to find online product reviews; in fact, you can do this right now by viewing Amazon: http://www.amazon.com and eBay: http://ebay.com

Apart from the two examples I have quoted above, there are a number of other choices to hand, such as conducting a standard internet search and using https://adwords.google.com/KeywordPlanner

Carrying out a standard internet search allows you the opportunity to determine what topics are already being used for articles etc.

In turn this will help you to determine how much competition there is out there regarding your topic.

Keyword is an expression given to a word, or sentence, which is actually typed into the Google search box by someone who is carrying out research on a given theme, on the Internet.

Keyword research tools help you to find these exact phrases you wouldn't have thought of, how those searches are being performed, and the number of searches carried out daily, monthly, locally and worldwide.

You can use these Keywords to help you find a hot 'topic' to write about and to form part of the 'Title' of your written work.

Using Keywords will help increase your targeted audience and Google rankings too.

People believe that keywords are not as important then they use to by and that was true a couple of years ago, but keywords still plays an important role in your websites SEO.

By covering a topic or story that's debating a hot 'topic', 'news release', product reviews, etc, you are bound to find success, just as long as the topic remains popular, or in demand.

You will find that this tactic is one of the easiest and quickest ways to get your content, name, or company distributed all over the Internet.

Tip1:

When it comes to writing compulsive, creative, and interesting content, you need to contemplate 'Writing from the heart'.

This is because people are bombarded daily by boring content, which very often reads and looks the same as the other boring content out there, which is freely available throughout the Internet to download...

How many top tips can there be written regarding the same subject?

There is a endless number of articles, news reports, product reviews, etc, flooding the Internet daily.

If you want yours to stand out from the crowd you need to make your content 'unique', 'interesting', 'engaging', 'exciting', 'fresh', and above all 'informative'!

"Write from a different angle, and write from the heart"

Tip 2:

I don't know about you, but I find it irritating to have my head full of following words and ideas, only to lose them before I can write them down.

So get into the habit of carrying a notebook with you at all times; now you can write down what you are thinking and never loss it.

Tip 3:

Ever writer has a time of day when their creative juices are following. Some work better in the morning, and some, like me, like to write late at night... Don't be afraid to experiment!

Tip 4:

Writing can get a little serious and lonely at times, so take time off and enjoy your life, your friends, or family, have some fun.

Tip 5:

It's very rear for a writer to be able to write 5000 words or more in any one sitting.

You should endeavour to write as many words as you can, don't think about the details; just get the story down on paper.

Then revisit your story to put things right... it's important not to get hung up on details until you have laid down your stories foundation.

Google's 'Duplication Penalty' Rule

There has been a lot of debate over the years regarding this ruling, does it really exist or has someone simply made it up?

Right from the beginning Google as made it its priority to gather and catalogue as much Internet content as possibly, regardless of its quality or uniqueness.

Google didn't realize that it was opening Pandora's Box, because the amount of rubbish and content duplication was ripe.

Anybody and everybody, took this information, put in their own links and distributed it all over the Internet.

This is the reason why Google is now looking to reduce the amount of duplicated content they allow into their index.

If you are aiming to create new content for your website, blogs, or content, then you must avoid filling it full of third party content.

This will only act to lower your chances of getting any high rankings in the Google's Serps (organic search listings).

Google can now recognize cloned or spun second-hand content and will ignore it... not very beneficial to your efforts.

Should you be caught leaching or scraping information on the Internet, and then submitting it throughout the Internet, then you may incur a *'Duplication penalty'*, which will be applied to your copy by Google, stopping you from achieving any of your original goals

Is it worth the trouble…well **no**, not when you can write original copy in the first place.

Listed below are some of my recommendations that will help you prevent people labelled with this rule:

- Avoid creating multiple pages using the same content, Sub-domains, or, domains with substantially duplicate content.

- Avoid **"cookie cutter"**. Affiliate programs tend to supply their members with the same duplicated content, and websites …thus they all end up contravening the rule.

- I would avoid submitting the same exact article to several directory sites at the same time, because the links they create today may very well disappear tomorrow.

- Get yourself a program like 'Plagiarism Checker'it sits on your desktop, and it's free. When you have some content check it with this software.

You should also avoid using any content spinning software. These programs are supposed to spin your content into hundreds of different versions, but not only do many not read right, but Google is now very adept at recognizing duplicate copy and will prohibit your activities.

I have personally tried many different ways to overcome this *'Duplication penalty rule'*, but it's always been detected and my work has been downgraded in the Google Serps.

The best way is to simply 'REWRITE' the content, and with practice you will be pleasantly surprised just how easy rewriting becomes.

More on Back Links

Many webmasters and business people use content to help create back-links to their websites.

The job of back-links is to entice their readers back to their Website's and very effective they are too.

In turn these back links help to push their website rankings higher in the Google research results.

You will however, need to overcome one problem when using article to build back links to your products or Websites.

Unfortunately, many article **'Directories'** will only allow you to put your links at the end of your article, this means that your readers **'Must'** read through to the end of your article, *before they are discovered by your readers*.

If you are a webmaster using this technique, then pay extra attention, because it is exceedingly imperative you go that extra mile to ensure that your content is interesting, easy to read, and contain some useful facts.

'How' do we Know if Our Content is Good or Bad

How can we ever know if our readers will find our content interesting? The fact is 'You won't' until you release them to the general public to read.

So your first consideration must be... "Do **You** like your own article"?

Sadly there isn't any real way of knowing if your readers will like what you have written until they respond to it.

That's **'Why'** I recommend you write about subjects you are enthusiastic about, first.

Belief in yourself and what you are writing, this is of parallel importance too. Of course this will come with time and practice, giving you an insider feeling of what will please others.

If your readers do respond you will have hit 'Gold', now it's a simple process of rinsing, repeating and profiting... *there is a lot of trial and error to writing an article.*

Proofreading

After you have fashioned your article, you will need to have it proofread, this is very, very, important.

It doesn't matter what you are planning to do with your content, selling them on, personal use, or submit them to article directories, you need to take the time to proofread your content first.

Carelessly written content turn off many Internet users… there is no quicker way to lose a reader than to have an article that is poorly written.

After you have methodically proofread and checked for spelling mistakes, I would recommend you re-examine it one more time, then get someone to read your article for you.

I know this is a lot of work, but after putting in the time to research and write the article, you don't want it to fail. Remember that your article, book, or sales content could be on the Internet for many years to come.

If they find your content full of spelling mistakes, bad grammar, tedious, boring, or dull, then you need to go back to the drawing board.

Your content must always be an easy read. It's not that hard to write a captivating article, but if it's too difficult to read, your reader will simply abandon their efforts.

When it comes to writing your content, write as if you were face to face with that person having a one-on-one conversation, building a glorious picture in their mind.

Don't Use to Many Technical Words

There's one other mistake that article writers tend to make, using big technical sounding words.

Unless, you are writing a technical tutorial, or if it's to

be read by specialists in the same field, don't get drawn into using words that most other people will find hard to understand.

This is no better than creating dry, boring content. If it's difficult for your readers to understand exactly what you mean, you run the risk of them being turned off your communication... *giving you the thumbs down.*

To write compelling, interesting, and captivating content, you must write from your heart. When writing your content eject just a little bit of colour, creativity and intrigue, it will uplift your content helping it go further.

Using creativity when writing can turn an otherwise boring article into a great one, and one your readers will not only enjoy reading, but one they will be happy to recommend and shear with others, spreading your ideas, messages, and links all-over the Internet.

When writing content, creativity is extremely important, even if you do not consider yourself to be a creative person. I recommended that you try sitting down and brainstorm your subject, this I found to be the best way to develop captivating article ideas.

Remember that your prospective customer started their research, because they were on the lookout for something.

They were attracted to your article or product, because they were already primed to do so. It shouldn't be a hard task to sell to them providing your content does its job.

Put Your Most Important Information First

When people go looking for a service, product, or information, unlike people who read books etc, they tend to *scan or glanced at the print, rather than read it.*

Most written essays or newspaper articles make their conclusions or main points, at the end of their article.

But on the Internet, it's important to get your main points across at the beginning of your text that's, because your reader knows exactly what they are looking for.

If you make this hard for your reader to achieve, they will move off to the next informative piece of content to find it.

Tip:

If your content is to be displayed on the Internet in a Website or Blog, then you need to make sure you put your main point(s) above the fold.

That's the area, which is displayed before you have to scroll down the page.

This is important, because people won't to see what your article or product is all about as soon as they land on your page.

If they can't they will more than lightly move on to somewhere else.

Don't Try Being or too Clever With Your Writing

I have written about this topic at length in my publication... 'Writing Copy That Sells - The Magical Power of Words', (30 rules to writing copy) and felt the need to write a quick word or two about this subject here... it contaminates most of the content I have read to date.

You should never lose sight of the reasons **'Why'** you are writing content in the first place. It's all about engaging your reader and then selling your goods or services to them.

Writing text that concentrates on trying to impress their readers, thinking that it will help sell their goods, is a destructive way to go.

It cannot work, because your targeted reader will be in a buying frame of mind and therefore, entertainment won't be at the top of their list.

Your customer isn't interested in you, they don't care how clever you are at writing, only the goods you have on sale, and *'What's in this for me'*!

***"Leave it out, because honestly it's not Clever"*!**

Before Submitting Your Content

There are a number of steps you should take before submitting your content to the Internet or your Website/Blog… don't wind up wasting an opportunity or your time.

The **5 steps** to writing effective content are:

1) Your first step is to 'Centre' on a topic you want to write about

For the best chance of success, write about a topic or an issue that is related to your topic. Any article might increase the traffic to your content, but you really want **'Targeted' traffic first, any other traffic is a waste of time.**

For example, if you are interested in selling a service, like an answering service, for example, then your article must centre around the benefits of using such a service.

2) Now you have established your chief topic, you now need to examine 'How' you will write your chosen subject

When I first started writing I found it a challenge to find a topic to write about, so now I create an outline.

An outline is a guide for you to follow, a road map if you will, bullet marking each step you should take next.

This should be built-up from the research you have

already carried out. An outline will not only help you know what to write, but it will likewise help to ensure you don't neglect any important information.

If however, you are still experiencing problems with writing your very own content, don't worry, help is at hand... see below for more information.

3) Writing Your Content

Your content must always help your reader. Writing about useful tips, how-to, advice, help, and making it easy to read, will keep your readers focus, and hopefully fascinated by your article.

But first a word of warning?

Be very mindful of using technical words that a majority of your readers may find challenging.

Tip:

Your first thought must be to produce content full of useful information, but do be cautious of providing too much?

It's very important to get your readers to click on the links in your content; this is your prime directive for your content.

If your article provides too much information, it may be possible for your reader to gleam enough information without necessarily visiting your website.

You should only detail enough information that will leave your readers wanting more ...**always**!!

4) What to do next

After compiling your article, it's absolutely essential for you to thoroughly proofread its content; this should be one of your golden rules.

People are really not very happy when reading content that is full of spelling and grammar mistakes.

Your content doesn't have to read like Queens English, but it must not contain any spelling mistakes.

I know from personal experience, when I first started to write content for my websites and blogs, that using online proofreaders can cost a small fortune, they can charge anything for proof reading 200 characters.

So if you have some content that runs into say 1000 characters, then it's going to cost you lots.

Tip:

If you don't have spare money for proofreading, then why not try copying your content into a text speaking software, you can find lots of free ones on Google.

In this way you can listen to your content through an unbiased voice, even though, the software generates a synthetic voice.

This will allow you to catch any possible spelling mistakes and sentences that don't really make sense, which will become obvious as the software works its way through your text.

Now you can submit your article to your chosen websites.

5) You may think that your work is now done, but it isn't

Creating content to advertise your website, blog, products, or goods, is a great way to generate traffic, but you will need to submit fresh content to the various websites on a regular basis.

You should set yourself a target like submitting at a bare minimum of five articles a month, or even more to your favourite websites.

This is to make sure that your new fans (readers) are always receiving new updated info to read and absorb, thus remaining loyal to you.

In point of fact, the more content you distribute the more links you can create.

I sincerely hope you enjoyed reading this book, and where able to take lots of valuable information too.

If you are looking for more information on writing please copy this link into your browser: http://mybooksupply.com/wp/creative-writing

By Judge J

More books from this author:

1) Lose weight Diet For Life

2) The Truth About Weight Loss And Diets

3) THE IMPORTANCE OF SUPPLEMENTS AND VITAMINS

4) Can Omega-3 Oils STOP Prostate Enlargement

5) Entrepreneurial Thinking - Sack Your Boss

6) Writing Copy That Sells: The Magical Power of Words

For more books and information please visit my Website: http://mybooksupply.com

Or my Amazon Authors Central page: amazon.com/author/judgej